# "Write Your Own" Writing Books for Kids

*Write Your Own Quest*

# Pick Your Own Quest Books

*King Tut's Adventure*

*Escape From Minecraft*

*Return to Minecraft*

*Minecraft The End*

*Trapped in A Fairy Tale*

*Dragon vs. Unicorn*

*Alice in Wonderland*

*Trapped in the 80s*

*Medusa's Head*

*Journey to the Center of the Earth*

*You are a Unicorn*

# WRITE YOUR OWN

# QUEST

## The Ultimate Guide to Writing Your Own Interactive Adventure

### BY
### P. J. HOOVER

ROOTS IN MYTH, AUSTIN, TX

Write Your Own Quest:
The Ultimate Guide to Writing Your
Own Interactive Adventure

"Write Your Own" Writing Books For Kids Volume 1

A Root in Myth Book
Austin, Texas
For more information, write
pjhoover@pjhoover.com

www.pjhoover.com

Paperback ISBN: 978-1-949717-34-1

For every kid who's
ever dreamed of going
on an adventure

# TABLE OF CONTENTS

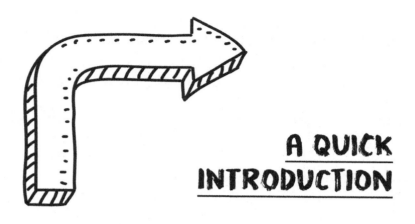

# A QUICK INTRODUCTION

ey, it's the author here, and whether you're a storyteller or not, this book is for you. If you're anything like me, when I was growing up, I did not want people telling me what to do. Whether it was my teachers, my sister, or my parents, if someone told me to do one thing, it made me want to do the exact opposite. I wonder if anyone actually realized that and used it to their advantage. Like did they ever say things like, "Hey Tricia, make sure you stay up late watching TV," which would have the hopeful intended effect of making me go to bed earlier? You know what? I'm going to have to ask my parents. Better yet, I'm just going to try that tactic on my own kids.

Another thing about me growing up? I did not want to be told what I "had" to read or write. Not in school. Not at home. I wanted to read fun, exciting books where I could go on epic adventures. Some of the time I was able to. I'd squeeze them in between the books I was required to read for school. And as for writing, I wanted to write fantasy stories where I could escape from the real world for a bit.

What's really cool is that now I get to read whatever I want. I also get to write whatever I want. And you know what I like to write?

## INTERACTIVE ADVENTURES!

Wait, you aren't quite sure what interactive adventures are? Don't worry. In this book we're going to talk about interactive adventures. We're going to learn how to write them ourselves. And we're going to discover that writing can (and should) be fun.

The best thing about reading an interactive adventure is that no one tells you what to do. You get to make the choices you want to make. The best thing about writing an interactive adventure is that no one tells you what to write. The story ideas are limited only by your imagination. There are infinite possibilities. Now let's get on with the book.

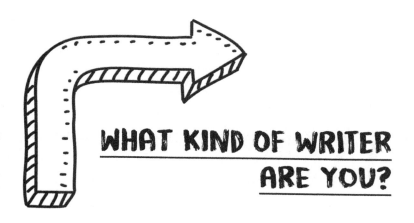

# WHAT KIND OF WRITER ARE YOU?

**Y**ou open this book and turn to the first page. You begin reading, and you find out you're about to embark on a great adventure. But wait . . . It only takes you a few words to realize that this isn't a story about monsters and adventure and daring deeds. This is a book about writing. You've been duped!

You know that there are two kinds of people in the world: those who love writing and dream of growing up to craft amazing stories, and those who would rather scrub toilets than actually sit down and write words. Which kind of person are you?

---

*If you love writing, turn to page 4.*

*If you would rather clean the toilet than write a sentence, turn to page 6.*

> (Reminder: You came here because
> you love writing.)

Welcome! I see that you are the type of person who loves to write. That's fantastic! Thanks for picking up this book. Maybe you're one of those people who wants to write as a hobby, and maybe you're one of those people who wants writing to be your job. Both are great options. When I started thinking about being a writer, I imagined sitting in my office all day long writing creative stories that people were going to be waiting on the edge of their seats to read. You know, kind of like the author of those *Percy Jackson* books. Or maybe like the *Harry Potter* author. That's how I imagined my life would be. It would be perfect. I would be famous. The world would be at peace because my writing would be so amazing. Oh, and I'd have a theme park created based on my books!

Guess what? That's not how things turned out. But that's okay. I love what I do.

One really important thing to keep in mind about being a writer is that everything you do will be different from anyone else. Your stories will be different. Your path to success will be different. And that's cool. It means that the future is unknown. But as long as you work hard at your writing and keep wanting to improve, success will wait for you!

Okay, now let's get back to the main story.

*Turn to page 8.*

(Reminder: You came here because you
aren't so fond of writing.)

I get it. You don't like writing. Don't worry. That's the
great thing about this book. It can really make writing fun.

Here's a secret about me. Okay, I guess it's not all that
secret because if you visit my website, it's on there in the
"About me" section. I never wanted to be a writer. Like
not ever. When I was young, the idea of writing enough
words to fill up page after page seemed impossible to me.
Writing one page of text felt like the most monumental
task in the entire world. So instead of being a writer or
having anything to do with writing, I took the easy way
out. I became an engineer.

Wait . . . an engineer?! But that is so different than
being a writer. (Also, it's not the easy way out.)

This is true. Writing and engineering are very different. Engineering is all about working hard and solving
problems and sticking with a project from start to finish.
And writing? Well, it's all about working hard and solving
problems and sticking with a project from start to finish . . .

Wait a second. Those sound like the same thing. Yeah,
sure, engineering has more math and science, and if you

like computer programming, it's a great career. But for both careers, it takes a lot of the same skills.

Oops, sorry. I'm getting off track. My point is that I didn't like writing. You don't like writing. I started liking writing. Maybe you never will. But the great thing about this book is that it makes writing fun. Way more fun than some of those essays you have to write for school.

Now that we've gotten that out of the way, let's get back to the main story.

*Turn to page 8.*

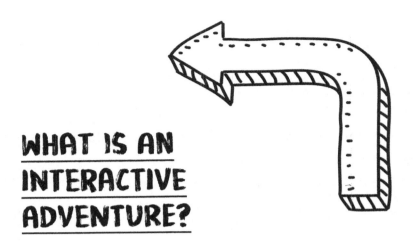

# WHAT IS AN INTERACTIVE ADVENTURE?

So anyway, here we are back at the main story. Tell me the truth. For whatever choice you just made, liking to write or rather be scrubbing toilets, are you curious to go back and read the other choice? If you want to, go ahead. Flip back a few pages. Then come back here.

I'll wait . . .

Okay, now that we've gotten that out of our systems, let's get on with the topic of this book, which is "Writing an Interactive Adventure." So, what exactly is an interactive adventure? Well, it's kind of like playing a video game on the latest, coolest console. You feel like you're part of the story. You make choices that determine what happens. You get so close to finishing the game. You defeat the final boss and win!

Or you die in the video game.

Either way, you restart the game and play it again.

Yep, that's pretty much exactly what an interactive adventure is. Except for when a book is an interactive adventure, there is no gaming console. There's no controller. But there are pages filled with lots of cool choices, and when you die, you get to start again. So, it's like a video game except inside a book.

It kind of goes like this. You open the book. You read a little bit of the story. Then it asks you to make a choice. And depending on what kind of choice you make, you turn to a specific page and the story continues. This is known as branching technology.

Branching comes from a term in computer science. It basically means that you're going down one path but something happens in the computer program that causes you to change directions. To go down another path. You've branched off.

No, we aren't writing computer programs in this book. That would be a whole different book. But . . . when you write an interactive story, you are kind of like the programmer for what is happening inside the book. You are writing code, but you're writing it as words. And instead of jumping to other places inside a computer's memory, you're having readers turn pages. That's kind of cool, right?

So why branching technology? It's not like the insides of computers have branches. Does your story have branches? Yes!

Let's look at it this way. The story can be visualized like a giant tree with branches shooting off in different directions. Your tree can be really simple, or it can be complex, with all sorts of branches sprouting off branches with green leaves at the end. We'll talk more about what your tree looks like later.

*That tree has a bunch of branches. It also looks a little spooky!*

In the meantime, let's wrap it up with a fun, cookie summary that shows perfectly what an interactive adventure is all about:

**AN INTERACTIVE ADVENTURE IS A STORY WHERE YOU MAKE CHOICES.**

- You have a choice where you must decide to eat one cookie or five cookies.
    - Do you eat one cookie?
    - Do you eat five cookies?

**THE CHOICES YOU MAKE DETERMINE WHAT HAPPENS NEXT.**

- If you eat one cookie, you feel fine.
- If you eat five cookies, you feel a little sick.

Oh, one more thing about interactive adventures? They're often (most of the time) written in second person. What does that mean? Keep reading to find out!

# COLOSSAL CAVE ADVENTURE

*Colossal Cave Adventure* was a computer program written between 1975 and 1977 and is the first known interactive story. In the game, you type in simple text commands to make choices. The goal of the game is to explore a cave filled with amazing treasure and wealth. It starts out like this:

**The Game >>>** YOU ARE STANDING AT THE END OF A ROAD BEFORE A SMALL BRICK BUILDING. AROUND YOU IS A FOREST. A SMALL STREAM FLOWS OUT OF THE BUILDING AND DOWN A GULLY.

**You type >>>** go south

**The Game >>>** YOU ARE IN A VALLEY IN THE FOREST BESIDE A STREAM TUMBLING ALONG A ROCKY BED.

So, as you go, you make choices, and things happen based on those choices. Also, the game has a lot of personality, just like your books and writing can have personality, too. Sometimes this is called "voice." If your teachers or editors have ever talked about "voice," this is kind of what they're getting at:

**You type >>>** go west

**The Game >>>** YOU FELL INTO A PIT AND BROKE EVERY BONE IN YOUR BODY!

**The Game >>>** NOW YOU'VE REALLY DONE IT! I'M OUT OF ORANGE SMOKE! YOU DON'T EXPECT ME TO DO A DECENT REIN-CARNATION WITHOUT ANY ORANGE SMOKE, DO YOU?

**You type >>>** yes

**The Game >>>** OKAY, IF YOU'RE SO SMART, DO IT YOURSELF! I'M LEAVING!

Look at that. The game is funny. And you can be funny in your writing, too. You can have voice!

*Colossal Cave Adventure* was written by a guy named Will Crowther for an old computer system called a mainframe. The computer weighed 12,500 pounds (which is over 6 tons—about the same as two elephants)!

Imagine a room filled with cabinets filled with computers. That's how big it was. All that just to play *Colossal Cave Adventure*. (Okay, not really. Mainframe computers did all sorts of other things. Gaming was just a fun extra thing people could do.) But the point is that you have no idea how slow and huge computers used to be!

You can still play *Colossal Cave Adventure* today. You can find it here online:

https://www.amc.com/shows/halt-and-catch-fire/
exclusives/colossal-cave-adventure

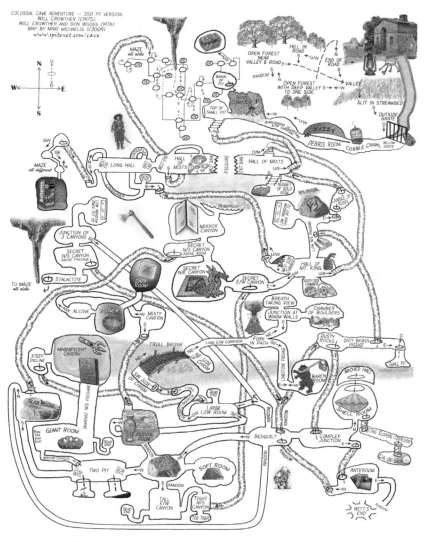

*The map of Colossal Cave Adventure (with spoilers)*

*Map copyright © Mari J Michaelis*

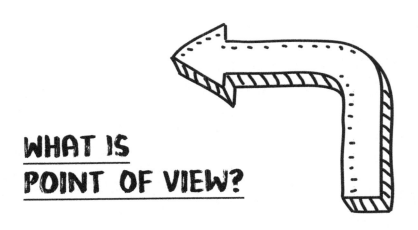

# WHAT IS
# POINT OF VIEW?

If you've ever had to suffer through a lecture about writing, then you may have heard the terms first person, second person, and third person. Let's look at some boring, classical books as examples.

Just kidding! No one wants to do that. Let's make it more fun!

However, if you do want to read some classical books for fun, go ahead. One of my very favorites is *The Twenty-One Balloons* by William Pene du Bois, which is a third person book that does a clever shift to first person when Professor William Waterman Sherman begins to tell his tale. But anyway, I'm getting off-track. Back to this book.

Let's say you're playing a video game like *Minecraft*. Or maybe it's *Doom Eternal*. Oh, or maybe it's *Mario Kart*. (I love *Mario Kart*, BTW. So. Much. Fun. Anyway . . .) Let's use *Minecraft* as an example.

## FIRST PERSON

You start the game and you're in what's called first person mode. You can't see yourself, and everything you see is as if you were viewing it out of your own eyes. Let's write a quick little snippet about your *Minecraft* experience.

*I stood near the base of a mountain. A cave entrance was right in front of me. This was perfect. I was going to find so much redstone. I would finally be able to power the rollercoaster I'd been building. But no sooner had I stepped into the cave when a Creeper appeared out of nowhere. He came toward me. I tried to back up, but my fingers got all jumbled on the controls, and . . . BOOM!*

So sad, right? The Creeper got you. Better luck next time. Anyway, that's an example of first person writing.

## THIRD PERSON

*Minecraft* lets you switch to third person mode. Lots of computer controls let you do this by pressing F5. If you've played *Minecraft*, you've probably done it. But how would the writing look different? Well, let's take a look. And just for simplicity, let's call ourselves "Steve."

*Steve stood at the base of a mountain. A cave entrance was right in front of him. He and his best friend Alex had been building a rollercoaster for the last week, and they needed more redstone. This cave was going to be the answer. Steve walked into the cave, ready to mine for the next two hours. There was movement in the corner of his eye. He turned, and coming around the corner, out of the dark, was . . . a Creeper! Steve tried to run, but there was a rock in his way. He tried to jump, but the Creeper was too fast. He turned back, and . . . BOOM!*

Poor Steve. Those Creepers are everywhere. And they are so annoying. Anyway, that's an example of third person writing.

## SECOND PERSON

Hey, maybe if Steve switched to second person mode, he'd be able to survive. And a quick note here that yes, I, the author, know you can't switch to something called "second person mode" in *Minecraft*. But that's the cool thing about writing and books. In writing and books, you can switch to second person mode.

If you notice in the previous examples, in the first person example, everything was "I did this" and "I did that." In the third person example, everything was "Steve did this" and "He did that." For second person, everything becomes "You did this" and "You do that."

Let's see how that looks.

*You stand at the base of a mountain. In front of you is a cave entrance you've never seen before. The last cave you mined didn't have any redstone, but you feel really good about this cave. And you definitely need redstone. You and your friend Alex have been building the most epic rollercoaster in the world, and you need to power it. You glance back and see the sun high in the sky. You should be safe. So, you step into the cave. It's so dark! You fumble around with your inventory to get a torch, but before you have time, a Creeper comes around the corner out of the dark. Oh no! If you die now, you are going to lose so much stuff. You try to equip your*

19

*sword so you can kill the Creeper, but your finger slips, and you equip a flower instead! The Creeper advances. He's only a couple blocks away. And then . . . BOOM! You die.*

Right. So, you still died. But do you see what we did there? We wrote the scene in second person. You were part of the story. And that's a big part of what makes a book interactive. As you read, you are part of the story.

**YOU go on the adventure.**

**YOU make the choices.**

**And if you make the wrong choice, YOU die.**

So, let's wrap it all up with a fun, cupcake summary:

- **First person:** "I am going to eat so many cupcakes today."
- **Second person:** "You want to eat cupcakes, but you know if you eat too many, you're going to feel sick."
- **Third person:** "Tricia snuck into the kitchen and ate four cupcakes. Then she shifted them around so it looked like none were missing."[1]

Now let's get on with what we need to write our own adventure.

---

1    I would never do that!

       Okay, fine, maybe I would.

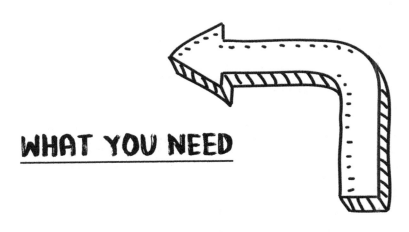

# WHAT YOU NEED

One of the questions I get asked the most about writing is "Do you hand write stuff or do you type?"

**Fact:** I type everything. My handwriting is awful. I never practice at it. It makes my hand cramp.

Here's the thing about writing, though. Every author you talk to will have a different answer to this question. You can do whatever works best for you! If you dream of sitting on a cozy sofa and writing your stories in a fancy notebook, then do it. If you want to use lined school paper and a clipboard to write your stories, you should. If you want to type on your phone, that's awesome. I, myself, have not mastered the art of thumb typing on my phone. I make typos all the time. And if you want to work solely on a computer or tablet, then that's a great choice, too!

Writing an interactive adventure comes down to two big stages:

1. Plan the story.
2. Write the story.

Whoa! That makes it sound so simple and easy. You know why? Because it is simple and easy! That's the great thing about writing interactive adventures. The method is straightforward. But . . .

You have to do the steps in the right order.

I know! You're so excited to get started writing. In your mind, you've probably already thought of some fun ideas of what to write. Maybe you've read an interactive adventure book, and you're ready to jump right in. I get it. I always feel that way. But here is a rule to live by:

## YOU HAVE TO PLAN FIRST!

Okay, now that we've gotten that out of the way, what do you need to plan your story?

## THE PLANNING STAGE

The first interactive adventure I wrote featured King Tut, ruler of upper and lower Egypt as he tried to figure out what was causing plagues and stuff in Egypt. It's lots of fun, has over 40 possible endings, and 84 boxes of writing.

Boxes of writing?

Right. Let me explain that.

Writing an interactive adventure can be thought of like a giant flowchart. If you've never used a flowchart yet in your life, don't panic. It looks something like this:

# A Basic Flowchart!

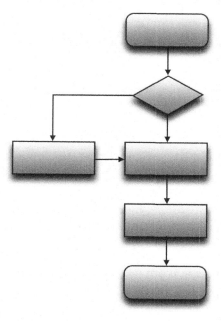

Each of those boxes is a "piece of writing." I refer to them as "boxes." Each of those arrows is a "choice." We'll talk more about the specifics of "boxes" and "choices" in a bit. But for now, when I refer to boxes or choices, that's what I'm talking about.

You know what, let's have a brief aside about flowcharts just to make sure we understand what is going on.

# WHAT ARE FLOWCHARTS?

Flowcharts can be used for all sorts of project planning. We're talking about using them to plan our interactive adventure, but they're also used for all those video games we talked about earlier. But don't think that flowcharts can only be used for practical things.

- You could use them to plan out what you are going to eat for your afternoon snack.
- You could use them to figure out why your Xbox remote doesn't work.
- You could use them for figuring out what game to play with your friends.

Here's an example flowchart. What snack are you going to have?

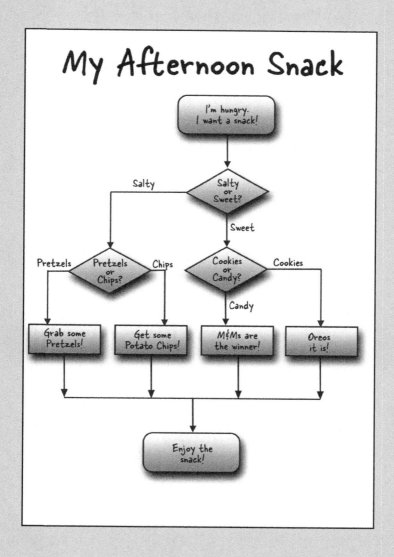

Flowcharts are basically a diagram that maps out a process. You start at the top, and you follow the arrows. You can have loops in them. You can have skip options. You can branch and merge your paths. The possibilities are endless. Grab a piece of paper where you can make your own flowchart. What process are you going to map out? Oh, and what snack are you going to have?

Do you feel like you kind of understand flowcharts? Good! Now back to what you need to plan your story. So, when I started writing my first interactive adventure story, I poured myself a giant cup of coffee and sat at the kitchen table. I had a few things (besides the cup of coffee):

- A sharp pencil
- An eraser
- A BIG piece of paper (or smaller pieces taped together)[2]
- A template for drawing squares
- A ruler (the side of the template can work, too)

That's all I needed to get started. We'll get to how to use all the stuff in a bit, but in the meantime, go collect these things. If you want to use a smaller piece of paper or a composition notebook for planning instead of the BIG piece of paper, you can do that, too, at least to get started. But as you write bigger and more complex interactive adventures, you will want more and more space.

---

2    It would only be fair to mention that I no longer plan my interactive adventures by hand. I use flowcharting software. There are all sorts of software programs you can use. I use one called *yEd Graph Editor.* But for starting out, planning by hand is the best way to go.

# THE WRITING STAGE

After you've planned your story, step two is to write it. For this step, you need whatever is going to make writing EASIEST for you. If writing on loose leaf paper is going to work best for you, then do that. If you want to type everything, then do that. There are no rules. There is no judgement. The main thing is to make it easy for yourself. You are in control of your writing.

For me, I use my computer and Microsoft Word. I should also mention that since I do my planning on the computer, I print out my giant flowchart before I start writing. That way I can mark stuff off as I write it. I also use a highlighter to color in boxes as I finish them, but if you've spent a lot of time planning your story, you may not want to mark on it. All that hand writing takes time and effort!

Okay, do you have all your supplies? Wait . . . here's a flowchart to summarize what we've just said. Go through the flowchart, and when you get to the end, move to the next section.

# Supplies Checklist

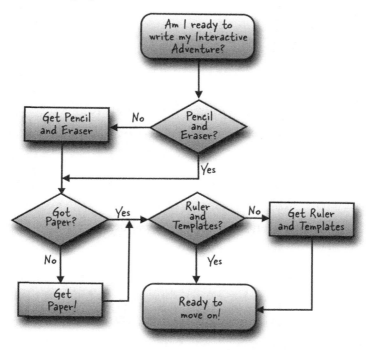

# WORD PROCESSORS AND
# QWERTY KEYBOARDS

You may use Microsoft Word or Google Docs when you're writing. These are pieces of software called "Word Processors." It's such a normal part of how we get work done, that we don't hardly think about it. But what about kids who lived ages ago, like in the 1960s or 1970s? Did they have word processors when they needed to work on school assignments or when they wanted to write books?

The short answer? Nope!

First, back in the old days, everyone wrote everything by hand. That makes my hand cramp just thinking about it. I have a hard time writing out my grocery list by hand!

Then, in 1868 a guy named Christopher Latham Sholes invented the first typewriter. Joy! People no longer had to write everything by hand. Now, instead of hands cramping from writing so much, fingers started cramping from mashing the keys on a typewriter. Typewriters soon became the new rage.

Have you ever wondered why they keyboard on a computer is so weird? Like why is the "A" next to the "S"? And why is the "Q" next to the "W"? It doesn't make any sense! But . . . there is a really good reason for it. There has to be, right?

When good old Christopher Latham Sholes first invented the typewriter, of course he put all the keys in alphabetic order. Why wouldn't he? It just makes logical sense. But as people tried it out, with some of the common keys spaced so close to each other, they would jam when people typed. So, what did he do? He shifted some of the most popular keys, like "E", "T", and "A" to the left hand. This slowed down typists and the keys stopped jamming. Viola! This was the creation of what we call the QWERTY keyboard!

There is absolutely no reason to still be using a QWERTY keyboard today when it comes to computer and cell phone keyboards, but that's just the impact the original typewriter has had on our society. So, the next time you're hunting and pecking for letters, you can thank Christopher Latham Sholes.

*Why did I type that sentence?*
*Search on the internet to find out!*

Okay, so what happened after the typewriter? When did word processors first come along?

Well, in the 1960s, people started messing around with them, but it was really in the 1970s when they took off. The first modern word processor was created in 1973. It was the "Vydec Word Processing System" and with it, you could even save your work to a floppy disk and print it. How cool! Everyone was going to take advantage of that.

Was it popular?

Well, it was a little expensive. Buying a copy of the Vydec software was $12,000 back then (that's like $60,000 in today's money)! I'm not sure about you, but I don't have a spare $12,000 (or $60,000) sitting around to spend on a word processor. I'm betting a lot of authors just kept on writing their books on typewriters. But this was a solid beginning for the word processor, and things only grew from there.

The first word processing system for personal computers came out in 1976. It was called Electric Pencil. I LOVE that name! WordStar came out in 1978, and then came Word Perfect and Microsoft Word in the early 1980s.

The point? The next time you have to write anything by hand, don't complain. The next time you don't know where a key is on the keyboard, don't get annoyed. Take that moment to be really thankful that you don't have to handwrite every single writing assignment that comes your way.

# COME UP WITH
# AN IDEA

You've made it this far! Or maybe you skipped right to this section. (Don't worry. No judgment.) Whatever the case, here you are. It is time to come up with an idea for your interactive adventure.

Here are quick summaries of some of the interactive adventure books I've written just to give you an idea of what's possible:

- You're King Tut, and you're trying to save Egypt from impending doom.

- You're playing *Minecraft* when you're sucked into the server. Can you escape?

- Your granny disappears into a closet. You follow after her and find yourself trapped in the land of fairy tales.

- Dragon and Unicorn both think they are the best, so they set up a series of contests to find out who really is the best.

Yes, these are really fun ideas, but you know what? I have SO MANY MORE ideas of stories I want to write! I could write interactive adventures all the time and be really happy doing it.

No, I'm not going to tell you my ideas. You have to come up with ideas on your own.

One of the best things you can do when you're trying to decide what to write about is to come up with not one idea, but five ideas. Yes, FIVE ideas. I know, it seems like a lot. But here's the thing about your mind. It likes to go to the easiest place first. And sometimes, the easiest place turns out to be the best place, but not always. Push your mind just a bit and see what you can come up with.

When you're coming up with ideas, there are a few things to keep in mind.

# CAN I WRITE A BOOK ABOUT MINECRAFT OR STAR WARS?

Everyone loves *Minecraft* and *Star Wars!*

Okay, fine, just because I love *Minecraft* and *Star Wars* doesn't mean that everyone does. So, let's amend our statement.

Lots of people love *Minecraft* and *Star Wars!*

I personally have written three *Minecraft* interactive adventures. They're fun to write and they're fun to read. But wait. I don't own the company *Minecraft*. I don't even work for *Minecraft*. How am I able to write a *Minecraft* book?

Some companies (like *Minecraft*) are pretty chill when it comes to people writing books inspired by their game. However, there are some rules they make people follow.

At the time I wrote my *Minecraft* books, the rules were things like:

- Make it clear that this is an "unofficial" *Minecraft* book (I do this on the cover and the copyright page).
- Do not start the title with "*Minecraft.*"
- Don't trash the game.

If you want to write a *Minecraft* interactive adventure, that's great! Just make sure to check what any updated rules are. You can probably find them on the *Minecraft* website.

What about *Star Wars?* Maybe you want to write an interactive adventure where Jar Jar Binks goes on an epic quest in search of an ancient artifact from Naboo. Sounds pretty cool, right? I'd read that.

Yeah, here's the thing. A company like Disney is not going to let you write a *Star Wars* book. If you want to write something to pass around class and share with your friends, that's great. But you won't be able to publish it. Sorry! This is just the harsh reality of the world of copyright.

If you want to write about some kind of brand, whether *Fortnight* or *Star Trek* or *My Little Pony,* check their copyright information on their website. They'll tell you there what is allowed and what isn't. Better to know BEFORE you write an entire book than after.

# CAN I WRITE ABOUT A REAL PERSON?

I wrote a book about King Tut. I didn't even ask his permission. I don't think he minded :)

But the whole thing does bring up the question about who you can and can't write about. Maybe you want to write an interactive adventure about Joan of Arc. Or Genghis Khan. Or Abraham Lincoln[3]. They won't mind. They won't even know, seeing as how they've passed on from this plane of existence.

For people that died a long time ago, there's no real problem having them be the main character of your interactive adventure.

---

3    I can kind of see it now. *"You're Abraham Lincoln. You put on your giant black top hat and your long black coat and head to the theatre. There's a play going on. Do you stay and watch? Or do you get a bad feeling and leave the theater?"*

What about someone who's died more recently? Can they sue you if you write about them? They can't, but their estates can. I'd suggest being careful with this. Some estates are really protective. (I can think of one in particular that I love. It's most famous book rhymes with "The Tobbit." I adore it, but I would never dare to write about it or its author.)

What about someone who's still alive? Like what about your next-door neighbor? Or your teacher? Or Miley Cyrus? You can write about them if you get their permission.

A good thing to keep in mind if you want to write about real people is to make sure they've been dead for a long time and that they don't have some estate that's going to come after you. That's an easy way to stay out of trouble.

All right. Do you kind of have a feeling for what you can and can't write about? Good. Now it's time to come up with your five ideas. Oh right, and keep them polite and inoffensive. It just makes everyone happier.

**WRITE DOWN FIVE IDEAS.**

Are you done? Do you like your ideas? Good! Now of these, which one do you love the most? Which one is really calling to you? Circle it, or draw a box around it or, if you have a highlighter, you can even highlight it.

Did you do that? Great! You now have a topic for your interactive adventure. There's one more thing to do before you get started. You need to come up with your one or two sentence summary of what the story is about. Remember my examples from earlier?

What is your story about? Write it down under your list of ideas.

All finished? Great! Now let's get started planning.

# FILL THE IDEA
# BUCKET

**Y**ou are doing so great! You now know what your interactive adventure will be all about. There are so many cool possibilities, and I bet you picked an amazing one.

Having a topic for your story is a really good start, but in order to have an interactive adventure, things have to happen. This is the part of the process people might call "brainstorming." (Cool word, right?). I like to call it "filling the idea bucket."

When authors brainstorm, they kind of let their minds run wild and come up with ideas. There is no judgment. There is no pressure. All you have to do in this stage is write down anything that pops into your mind about what could happen in the story.

So, what do I mean by ideas? Well, let's say you're writing a story about fairy tales. In order to come up with five "ideas" for your fairy tale interactive adventure, you could list out five fairy tale options. Like:

- Jack and the Beanstalk
- Hansel and Gretel
- Cinderella
- Little Red Riding Hood
- Snow White

There. That's five ideas of paths you could take in your fairy tale story. These go into your "idea bucket."

Okay, I know what you're thinking. Fairy tales are easy. You have a much more complicated story. Fine, let's look at something different.

What about book where Dragon and Unicorn both think they are the best. They decide to have a series of contests to see who is actually better. If you were writing a story about two creatures having a contest, when you brainstorm ideas, you could come up with five contests.

- Roller Skating
- Baking a cake
- Building a sand castle
- Running a race
- Drawing a picture

There. Five contests that Dragon and Unicorn could have to see who is better. Put them in your "idea bucket."

Are you starting to get the feel for what we're doing? An important thing to keep in mind is that you do not have to use all these ideas. This is just your "idea bucket." As you're planning your story, you can pull an idea from the bucket and decide if you want to use it or not. And with this in mind, it's way better to come up with more ideas rather than less.

So, are you now ready to brainstorm? Are you ready to create ideas to put in your "idea bucket?" Good! Now let's do this!

As a refresher, what is the subject of your story? Write it down again at the top of a new page.

Perfect! Now spend some time coming up with a bunch of ideas. Under your story topic, write down as many ideas as you can in five minutes. Then step back and admire your work.

Look at that. You've filled your "idea bucket." Now it's time for the really fun part.

# COME UP WITH EIGHT POSSIBLE ENDINGS

Filling the "idea bucket" is fun and all, but maybe the best thing about writing an interactive adventure is dreaming up all the horrible awful ways your reader can meet their end. Wait, what? you might be thinking. Horrible ways readers will meet their end? That doesn't sound good at all. Do I have to do that?

The short answer is "no."

The longer answer is "no, but it's kind of fun, so why would you not want to?"

Let's break this into two parts, shall we?

First, what if you are a peace-loving kind of person and you don't want anyone to meet a horrible end? Fine. Your interactive adventure will not be so much about the endings as it will be about the stuff that goes on before the endings. Here are two examples I'll give you.

You decide to write a book where a Pirate and a Princess both think they deserve a treasure and they're determined to have a contest to prove who should get it. In each path the storyline takes, the Pirate and the Princess face different challenges. At the end of each path, someone will win, either the Pirate or the Princess. Oh, right, there could be a tie. Neither the Pirate nor the Princess are meeting some horrible awful end, and that's good. The story doesn't really call for it. But . . . that doesn't mean that your endings have to be boring. You can still have a ton of fun with each path. Here are a few ideas you could go with:

1. The Princess wins but the Pirate steals the treasure and sails away.

2. The Pirate makes such a great cake that the Princess suggests they just share it and watch their favorite TV show together instead of continuing the contest.

3. The sand castle contest is about to end when a bunch of kids run over the sand castles, destroying them, so no one can be a winner.

These are just ideas! The point is that endings can still be different and cute even when horrible death and destruction are not involved.

You decide to write a story about traveling into a deep cave and trying to find your way out. Maybe, in every single ending, your reader will find the way out. That's fine. But you could mix it up a little. You could make it a time-traveling cave, where every path you take leads to a different part of time. Here are some possible endings if this is the case:

1. You are trapped in the time of dinosaurs.
2. You travel to the future and blast into outer space on a spaceship.
3. You end up wandering the cave forever, looking for your way out.

None of these ends with death and destruction, but they're still fun. So, if you don't want your reader to die in horrible awful ways, it's definitely possible.

We've gone over some possibilities if you're the peace-loving type. What about if you don't mind a little fatality in your stories? What you need to do is come up with some great and happy ways for your story to end, but you also need to come up with a balanced amount of horrible, awful endings. Whatever you come up with, it's got to fit with your story. For example, if you're living the life of King Tut, then it is very likely that one of your ends could be getting eaten by a crocodile. After all, there are crocodiles in the Nile River which runs right through Egypt.

For a Fairy Tale interactive adventure, however, getting eaten by a crocodile isn't such a likely end. So, what you need to do is come up with a list. Let's go with eight possible endings. And since it's good to have balance, let's say there are four "positive" endings and four "negative" endings. We'll use Fairy Tales as our example.

## FOUR "POSITIVE" ENDINGS

- In the Three Little Pigs, you escape getting eaten by the big, bad wolf, and enjoy wolf stew for dinner over the nice fire you built.

- In Jack and the Beanstalk, you defeat the giant and become the ruler of his sky kingdom.

- In Hansel and Gretel, you push the witch into the oven and then gorge yourself by eating the entire house made of candy.

- In Snow White, you decide living with the seven dwarves is much more fun that trying to be some boring princess, so you decide to stay with them and get the most out of life for a while.

*Cinderella could vow to never get married.*

## FOUR "NEGATIVE" ENDINGS

• In The Old Woman Who Lived in a Shoe, you are stuck babysitting all her kids forever.

• In Little Red Riding Hood, you get eaten by the wolf.

• In Goldilocks and the Three Bears, Baby Bear wants you to be his playmate and never lets you leave.

• In Sleeping Beauty, a prince is supposed to kiss you to wake you up, but he gets a better offer and you are stuck sleeping forever.

Right?! It's kind of fun. Now it's your turn. And remember, nothing you are writing now is set in stone.[4] This is all still part of the brainstorming process.

On your piece of paper, write down four "Positive" Endings.

When you finish that, write down four "Negative" Endings.

If you want to come up with more than eight possible endings, do it! Or more. Have fun with it. And when you're done, it's on to coming up with your first choice.

---

4    Which is a fancy way of saying that anything can be changed

# THE CAVE OF TIME

*The Cave of Time* was the very first interactive adventure in the *Choose Your Own Adventure* series. When I was in sixth grade, my school had a book fair, and the only books I wanted were the first six *Choose Your Own Adventure* books. I loved the concept, and I was hooked. Just a note that I still have my original copies of these books!

*The Cave of Time* by Edward Packard was first published in 1979. That is ages ago. In the book, you are a kid who's riding a bike when you find a cave that you've never noticed before. So, what do you do? You go inside! Sure, maybe this isn't the best idea. (Kids, don't go in dark caves alone.) But if you don't go into the cave, there will be no adventure. And if you don't want adventure, then maybe reading an interactive adventure book isn't the best idea. Anyway, you go into the cave, and this is where the time travel and the adventure starts.

Before I wrote my own first interactive adventure, I mapped out *The Cave of Time* so I could learn more about how the whole process was done. If you have an interactive adventure already sitting around your house, this is a great activity to do. In *The Cave of Time*, there are 40 endings. If you want the statistics, 16 are bad, 18 are good, and 6 are kind of in the middle. It's a nice balance because there's a lot of hope for the reader. You don't want the reader to meet their end with any choice they make. And seeing as how *The Cave of Time* is still in print today, over forty years later, it must be doing something right.

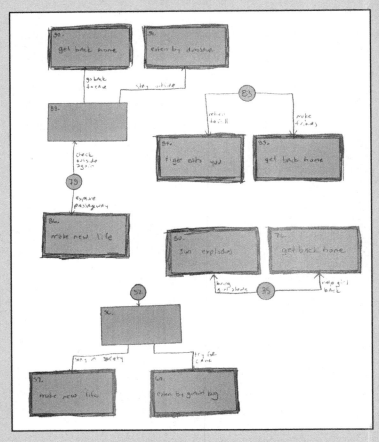

*Sample endings from The Cave of Time*
*(mapped out by Yours Truly)*

# IT ALL BEGINS
# WITH A CHOICE

**E**very great adventure begins with a choice. A single choice! An interactive adventure is no different. In fact, the entire story is told as a series of choices, but the first choice is the most important. First off, it's the first one you need to write, and second off, it sets up so much about the main character. We'll get into way more about this in the actual writing stage. For now, we're going to get started!

A good starting choice in an interactive adventure should have two solid yet different paths, such that each path offers a completely different opportunity. Let's look at a couple examples.

Suppose you're reading an interactive adventure where you're playing the role of King Tut, and you start out in the throne room. You (as King Tut) are listening to people complain about their problems. One crazy guy comes in and tells you that the Nile River has turned red.

**YOUR TWO CHOICES ARE:**

• Stay in the throne room and listen to more people complain about their problems.

• Go check out the Nile River.

We'd draw our first choice with boxes and lines like this:

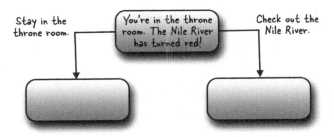

Fun, right? Let's look at another example.

You're sitting in a rocking chair waiting on hot chocolate when your granny disappears into a closet. You go in the closet to check on her, but inside the closet is a whole other world. It's the world of Fairy Tales! You see a fancy castle ahead of you in the distance. But off to the left is a dark forest.

**YOUR TWO CHOICES ARE:**

- Go check out the fancy castle. They might have fancy snacks.
- Head to the dark forest.

We'd draw our first choice with boxes and lines like this:

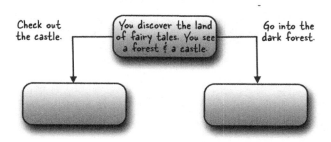

Check out the castle.

You discover the land of fairy tales. You see a forest & a castle.

Go into the dark forest.

Okay, one more, only because they are fun. And also, because this one is a little different.

You are writing about an epic contest between two characters, a Pirate and a Princess. Your first choice is simple.

## WHO DO YOU WANT TO PLAY AS?

- Play as the Pirate.
- Play as the Princess.

We'd draw our first choice with boxes and lines like this:

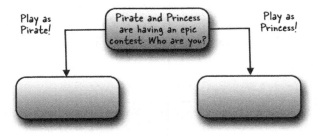

I bet you have the idea and are ready to come up with your very first choice. Draw some boxes on your piece of paper that look like this.

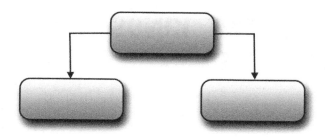

Now fill them in. Use a pencil in case you change your mind. If you want to come up with different first choices, draw some more boxes and start over. Remember, this is your very first choice. There will be many more. Also, here's where the ruler and the template come in handy. If you use the template for drawing squares and the ruler for making lines, your adventure will look so much better. You can frame it when you're done. Also, if you make a mistake, use your eraser. That's why we're writing in pencil.

Go ahead. Have at it!

Are you done? Way to go! You have officially started planning your interactive adventure. Now let's get this party started!

# DIFFERENT KINDS OF PATHS

I know! You're ready to start planning your story. Heck, after writing this guide, I'm ready to start planning another interactive adventure. They're so much fun! We're almost ready to get started, I promise. But first . . .

**LET'S HAVE ANOTHER SNACK.
I'M GETTING HUNGRY.**

What if this time, when we make our snack choice flowchart, we give ourselves the option to have TWO snacks? Sometimes I want a salty AND a sweet snack. Let's do that. What if we also want more choices than just pretzels and chips for our salty snacks? What if we want popcorn as a choice, too?

Here's what our flowchart would look like.

# My 2nd Afternoon Snack

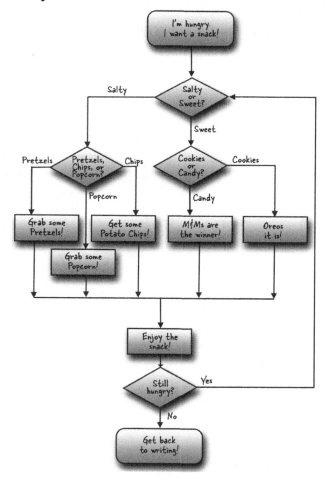

Yum! Have a snack. Have two. Then let's get back to work.

When planning your interactive adventure, you have to understand the various possibilities of what you can do with your story. What I mean by this is that the story isn't linear. It's branching. Remember the tree from earlier? And in branching storytelling, there are options. Let's go over them.

*Some branches of the tree split off into two new branches.*
*Others split off into three (or more)!*

## BASIC TWO-CHOICE BRANCH

You come to a fork in the road. There are two ways you can go. Do you go right or left? Into the dark cave or follow the river? Talk to the crazy old lady or walk away as fast as you can? You have two choices and you have to take one. This will likely be your most common branching option.

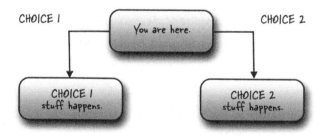

*There are two possible ways to go.*

## THREE-CHOICE BRANCH

Sometimes when you come to an intersection, there are three ways to go.

*You're in the fairy tale world, and there are three houses in front of you: one made of straw, one made of sticks, and one made of bricks. In which one do you hide from the big, bad wolf?*

*You come to a house and inside are three beds. You want to take a nap. Which bed do you take a nap in: the big one, the medium one, or the small one?*

It's fun to throw a three-choice branch into your interactive adventure. You just may not want too many because of something called exponential growth. I'll talk about that in a bit.

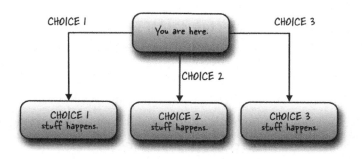

*There are three possible ways to go.*

## NO CHOICE

Sometimes when you're writing an interactive adventure, you may want to add a "turn of the page" even when there is no choice to be made. Why? Well, maybe you're trying to build suspense. It could be something like this.

*At the end of the tunnel, you see the flickering of torchlight. You hear low voices. Someone is around the corner. But who? Whoever it is could be dangerous, or they could offer you food and water. You think for a second about turning around, but the monster is still back there. Turning around is not an option. There is no choice but to move forward and see who is around the corner.*

### Turn the page.

So, in this way, you do it to build a little suspense.

Another case where you might want to do it when there are a lot of words that you've written, and you want to break them up a little. After all, one of the best things about reading interactive adventures is that you don't have to read a ton of words all at one time.

Whatever the case, "no choice" is a path option you can use in your interactive adventure.

*There is only one possible way to go.*

## MERGING PATHS

If you're looking for something a little more challenging when you're writing your interactive adventure, merging paths is a fun choice. Why would you do this? For one, it might make logical sense. Imagine you drew out the setting of your interactive adventure (which is a great idea, BTW). What if it looked like a city map, something like this?

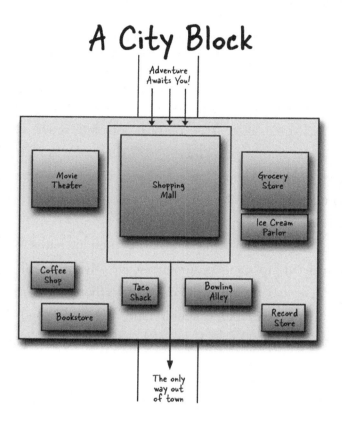

A City Block

Adventure Awaits You!

Movie Theater

Shopping Mall

Grocery Store

Ice Cream Parlor

Coffee Shop

Taco Shack

Bowling Alley

Bookstore

Record Store

The only way out of town

Your story could start at the place marked "Adventure Awaits You" and have branching paths. Maybe you want coffee. Maybe you want ice cream. Maybe you just want to get through town. But when the two paths have gone forward a bit, they once again come to the same street.

They merge. You take that path because it's the only way to get out of town. But when writing merging options this way, you have to be careful. (I'll talk more about this in a second.)

What's another reason you might have merging paths? Well, when you read the section on "Exploding Exponents," you'll see that as you plan your interactive adventure, the number of "boxes" you need to write can get pretty big. Including some merging paths is a clever way to reduce the number of future options you have to take care of.

Okay, back to being careful with merging paths. When you decide to merge your interactive adventure, all of a sudden, two options are coming together. That's means that for the current moment in time, there are two possible things that could have happened in the past. Like imagine the city block again, but with dangers!

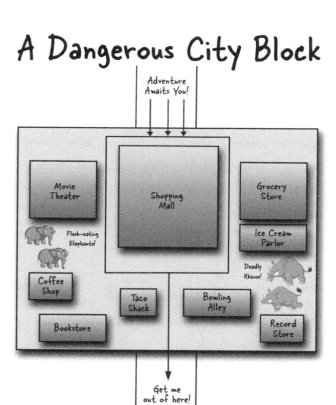

On one path you are chased by flesh-eating elephants. On the other path you are chased by deadly rhinos. Yikes! Both are scary situations. When your two paths merge back into one, and you begin heading forward, you want to avoid saying things like, "Wow, those flesh-eating elephants almost caught me!" because what if the reader had come

71

from the deadly rhino path? They would have no idea what you were talking about, and they would assume that you, as the writer, made a mistake (which in fairness, you did).

Don't let this scare you! I'm certainly not saying that you can't have merging paths. Just if you do, keep your language kind of generic, and you should be good to go. And by "generic" I mean that you could say something like, "That was about the scariest thing ever! I'm glad that's far behind me," instead of calling out the rhinos and elephants specifically.

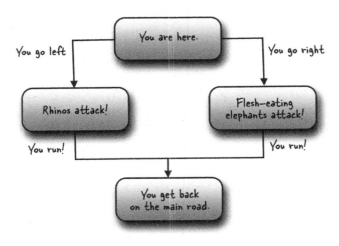

*Different paths can lead back to the same place.*

*Sure, they may look cute, but can you really trust them?*
*Danger could be everywhere.*

## CIRCLE-BACK

Have you ever seen the movie *Groundhog Day?* (If not, you should.) Each day, the main character wakes up and the same day repeats itself over and over again. This is called a "loop."

Like merging paths, loops are a little more complicated to plan and write.

You don't want to have loops all over the place in your interactive adventure. After all, part of the fun is when you reach one ending, you turn back to the beginning of the book and start over. But having maybe one or two loops written into your story can be a fun and clever way to entertain your reader. In fact, many readers of interactive adventures will actually look for loops in stories.

Here's an example of when you might have a loop.

*Imagine you enter a haunted house, and you have a choice. You can decide to go upstairs or you can decide (for some crazy reason) that you want to go down the dark staircase into the creepy basement.*[5]

---

5    Why do people in horror movies go into creepy basements!? It makes no sense!

74

*You go into the creepy basement (why!). Okay, so there you are in the creepy basement. There are all sorts of creepy things around (like clowns and dolls. Hey, don't blame me if you're scared. You're the one who went into the creepy basement.). You have to figure a way out of here.*

*In one direction is a door and in another direction is a set of stairs leading up. You take the stairs and . . . you're outside! Yay!*

*Ahead of you is a house. You dash toward it. It looks haunted but you still go inside. Once inside you see a staircase leading up and a staircase leading down into a creepy basement. This time you go up the stairs. You have learned your lesson. No more creepy basements!*

Oh, and keep in mind these are all choices you would be making. All of this would NOT happen in one story box.

This is just an example of how you might loop back to a previous part of your interactive story. It's kind of like playing a game of *Chutes and Ladders*. If you fall through a chute, you end up backtracking (normally not a good thing). You have to repeat steps, and hopefully you'll do better the next time and not fall through the chute.

When you use circle-backs, like with the merging paths, make sure you keep in mind previous paths that led here. It can get a little tricky, because, you know, once you're upstairs, no matter how you got there, you can't say things like, "Hope I don't see the dolls again!"

Once again, I'm not saying you can't do it. Just be aware and be clever.

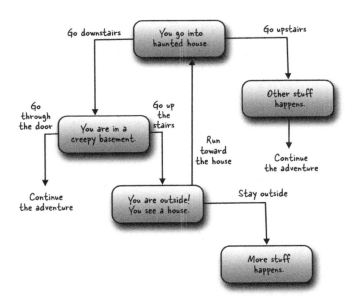

*You can repeat the same path.*

## TURNING BACK

Nope, turning back is not an option. What kind of adventure would it be if you could just turn around if you didn't like how the story was going? That's not how life is, and it's not how interactive adventures go.

Wait a second . . . That feels kind of harsh. Just because it's not normally done this way doesn't mean that you couldn't try something new. After all, in video games, if a ton of enemies show up, sometimes you can turn and run away from them. I don't write "Turn Back" options in my interactive adventures, but maybe you want to. You are the writer! You can do whatever you want.

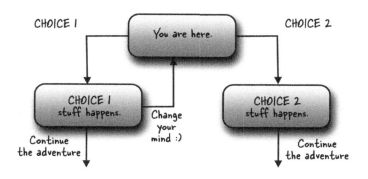

*There can be do-overs if you want!*

## AND NOW A BRIEF SNACK . . .

So back to our second snack flowchart. Let's look at it and label our options with what we've learned. It would look something like this.

# My 2nd Afternoon Snack

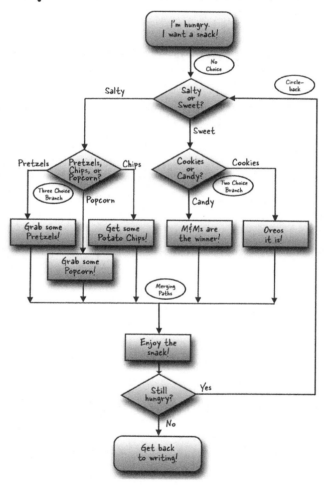

Now have another snack and keep reading!

# EXPLODING EXPONENTS

If you look at a tree, sprouting off the main trunk may be three branches. That's not a lot. But each of those branches may have three more branches sprouting off it. And those might have three more sprouting off them. Let's look at that.

- Level A: 3 branches
- Level B: 9 more branches
- Level C: 27 more branches

Just at the end of three levels, there are now 39 branches on the tree! If you were writing a story and that's what your story looked like, you'd have to write 40 story boxes already. That adds up quickly. This is what exponents are all about. It's called exponential growth, and this is one reason you may not want too many three-choice branches in your story.

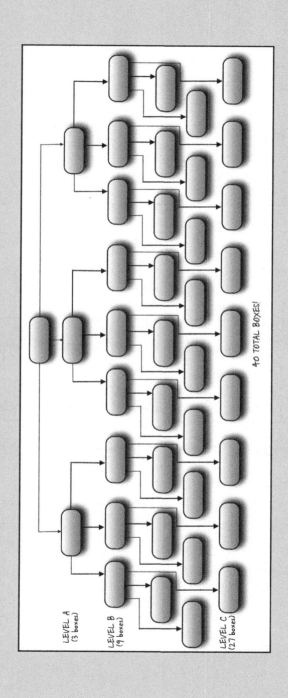

LEVEL A
(3 boxes)

LEVEL B
(9 boxes)

LEVEL C
(27 boxes)

40 TOTAL BOXES!

Okay, fine, you say. You decide to use only two-choice branches in your story. What does that look like?

- Level A: 2 branches
- Level B: 4 branches
- Level C: 8 branches

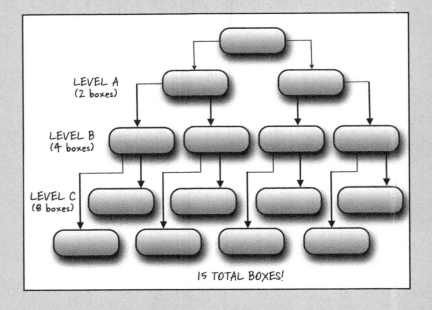

So, at the end of three levels, you have 14 branches or 15 story boxes to write. It's much more manageable. Make your writing life easy. Don't create too many branches!

# A Chess Story

There's a fun story that may or may not be true about the guy who invented the game of chess. It goes something like this.

A really smart guy invented the game of chess and presented it to the king. The king had been playing the same game of *Uno* for the last month and was so sick of it that he was about to have his opponent executed just so the game would end. So, this inventor showed the king the game of chess, and the king was overjoyed! He decided he wanted to reward the inventor and asked the inventor what he wanted.

---

*Turn the page to hear what the inventor's response was.*

The inventor said:

*"I'll take one grain of wheat for the first square on the chess board, two grains for the second square, four grains for the third square, and so on. So for each square, I want double the grains of wheat as the square before it."*

The king laughed at what a simple reward this was and agreed. After all, one and two grains of wheat is nothing. However . . . this is exponential growth. These grains of wheat can add up quickly.

| SQUARE | GRAINS | TOTAL GRAINS |
|--------|--------|--------------|
| ONE | 1 | 1 |
| TWO | 2 | 3 |
| THREE | 4 | 7 |
| FOUR | 8 | 15 |
| FIVE | 16 | 31 |
| SIX | 32 | 63 |
| SEVEN | 64 | 127 |
| EIGHT | 128 | 255 |

After just one row of the chess board, we are up to 255 grains of wheat. Still not a lot. But here's the thing. There are 64 squares on a chess board, and if you keep doing this (we're not going to show it here), there will be:

**18,446,744,073,709,551,615**
**(eighteen quintillion, four hundred forty-six quadrillion, seven hundred forty-four trillion, seventy-three billion, seven hundred nine million, five hundred fifty-one thousand, six hundred and fifteen)**
**grains of wheat**

*Wow!*

Okay, when the king realized this, he was not pleased. Not at all. And so the story concludes in one of two ways:

- He has the inventor executed.
- He makes the inventor his highest-ranking advisor.

**The moral of the story?** When you're dealing with exponents, they can add up quickly!

**The second moral of the story?** Don't try to fool the king. You might get your head chopped off!

# PLAN YOUR ADVENTURE

You are ready to plan your story. Like really ready! Yes, we've come up with an idea. We've come up with possible endings and a list of things that can happen. We even have our first choice. Now we get to plan EVERYTHING!

Keep this is mind: For an interactive adventure, the planning is the most tedious part. Really! The writing is not the hardest part. It's the planning, and this is because you actually have to think while you plan.

Oh, but it's also fun. It's like writing a video game!

Anyway, let's get started.

The first thing you need to do is start drawing your boxes. You can use some of the fancier branching options that we talked about before, or you can just go with simple basic two branches. Grab a giant piece of paper. Use your square-drawing template and your ruler. You can also download a template from my website.

My website:

## www.pjhoover.com

The template I've created is for a basic eight-ending story.

In your very top box, write your starting point. This is just a short description. You aren't writing text here. For example, if you were writing an interactive story about *Minecraft*, you could write:

*"Playing Minecraft. Get sucked into server."*

Now, on the two arrows shooting off it, write your two choices. Again, for planning purposes, keep it simple. You could write:

*Head toward mountains.*
*Head toward forest.*

This is what it would look like:

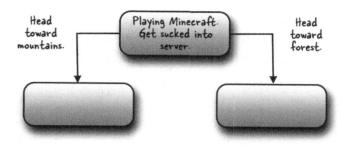

You've now officially planned your first choice. Now just keep going.

Sometimes I jump around a lot when I'm planning, and sometimes I fill in one entire path before going back to a different one. Do whatever works for you. If you need to add more boxes, do it. If you need to end a path earlier, you can do that, too.

A clever way to keep track of things: I mark my ending boxes differently. If I'm drawing them on paper, I double-outline the box. If I'm using flowcharting software, I make them another color. This helps me keep track of which paths I've finished. In the example below, the endings have the dashed outlines.

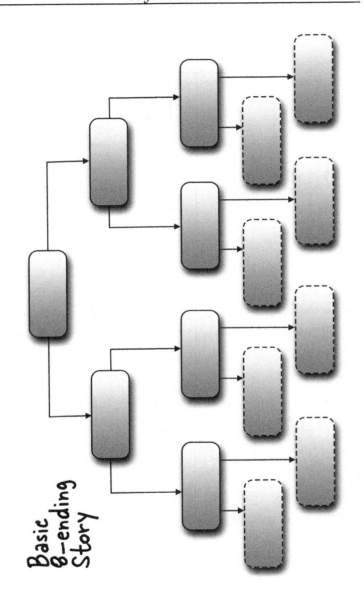

Basic
8-ending
Story

Okay, now go plan your story. I'll wait here.

Are you done? Great! There is one more thing to do before you should start writing. You need to number your boxes.

Start at 1 and number each of your boxes. The top box is 1, but then from that point, number them however you want. I tend to keep my somewhat linear, so the reader isn't often turning backward in the book, but that's just how I like to do this. You can put the numbers wherever you want. You'll use these numbers when you write your story.

When you are done, your finished, planned story should look something like this:

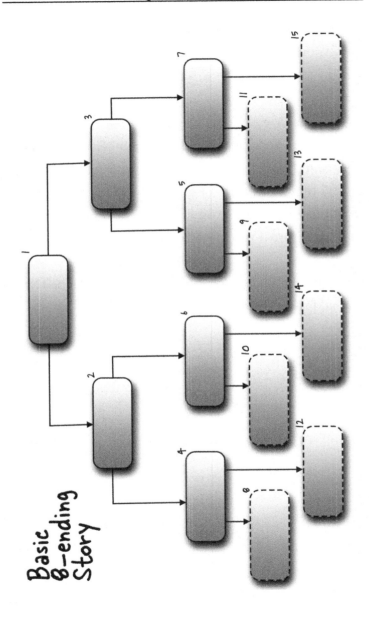

Basic
8-ending
Story

Congratulations! You have planned your interactive adventure. Why not celebrate? A Hershey's Kiss? A nice apple? A big glass of lemonade? Or maybe just give yourself a high five. And now, you are now officially ready to start writing your interactive adventure.

# STARTING YOUR STORY

**W**ondering how to start your story? The first thing you have to do is to set up the idea of an interactive story for the reader. Not all readers are familiar with this type of story. People are used to reading books from the beginning to the end, so you have to let them know this is different. If someone reads your interactive adventure from beginning to end, they are going to get very confused. Do what you can to avoid this!

Here's one generic option for starting. I call it:

BOX 0

## BOX O SAMPLE

Don't read this book like other books. If you read this book from front to back, nothing will make sense. But if you follow the instructions on each page, the story will come to life. Okay, the thirty-one stories. Because that's how this book works.

There are thirty-one different stories inside. Read the words on the page. When it tells you to make a choice, you turn to the page that it tells you to turn to. One thing you have to keep in mind. You can't turn back.

If you're expecting every story to end with sunshine and rainbows, you might as well put this book down. Sure, sometimes you might get to the end just fine. But other times . . . well, my friend, remember, danger is everywhere. With over thirty possible ways to finish the story, you know you're going to fall into a lava pit or something equally horrible at least once.

*If you dare, turn the page.*

So obviously, you'd need to change a couple things here. Like your story is going to have a different number of endings than my story did. And your story might not have a lava pit as a possible danger. And of course, you can't copy it word for word because that would be something called copyright infringement. But I do want to point something out about the above story start. Look how short and to the point it is!

Starting your story can be really hard. I've been writing for years now, and every time I'm getting ready to start a new story, it's difficult to get motivated. It feels so daunting, like I have such a big task in front of me.

Do you ever feel this way about your writing?

If you do, remember that's basically how tons of people feel (including me). So, here's my secret to getting started:

### WRITE ONE PARAGRAPH.

Make that your goal. It's a small goal, but it's a great goal! If you set your writing goal small, then it's so much easier to do. And if you do write one paragraph, you may feel motivated enough to write a second. And then a third.

And the best thing about an interactive adventure? Before you know it, you have one "box" done. Each box doesn't have a lot of words, but when you finish even the first box, you are well on your way. You have started the book, and you're bound to finish.

So, get started. Write that first paragraph. Let's go!

# WHAT IS COPYRIGHT INFRINGEMENT?

Copyright infringement isn't good. In fact, it's really bad, and you can get into a lot of trouble for doing it. But wait, you aren't sure what copyright infringement is? Well, it's basically when you copy someone else's work. (And if you try to pass it off as being your own, then that's something also really bad called plagiarism.)

Let's pretend you take the introduction paragraphs I wrote and you copy them without my permission. That's copyright infringement. (And no, you DO NOT have my permission to use them). And worse, if you try to pretend you wrote them, then you are plagiarizing my work. Don't do that!

So, what trouble can you get into for copyright infringement? You might just get a slap on the wrist, but you might have to pay a fine (which is a lot of money), or you could even go to jail. Do you want to pay lots of money or go to jail? No? I didn't think so. So don't copy other people's work without their permission. It's that simple.

*Do the right thing!*

# MAKE A PLAN AND DO IT!

Y ou have written your first box. This is amazing and awesome and also always a good time to celebrate. Now count up how many boxes you have to write. If you've gone for the basic two-choice branching, eight-ending setup, then you have fifteen more boxes to write (since the first one that you just wrote was an introduction to the book). If you've decided to go for sixteen possible endings, then add in sixteen more boxes for a total of 31 more. Don't panic over how many you have left to do. Just make a goal.

Setting a goal to write four boxes a day is a great plan. At four boxes a day, your fifteen boxes will take four days to write. If you've gone for sixteen possible endings and have 31 boxes to write, you have about eight days of work ahead of you.

Think about that for a moment. In about a week, you can have this book written! The key, however, is that you have to stick to it, even when you don't want to.

I recommend making some kind of goal chart. On the next couple pages are examples of an eight-ending and a sixteen-ending goal chart. For each "box" that you write, put a star sticker on there (or just draw a star; use fun colored gel pens or Sharpies if you want). Look, I even added the initial "getting started" box that you already wrote (what I called Box 0). Go ahead. Put a star on it. You deserve it!

# 8-Ending Goal Chart

| | |
|---|---|
| BOX 0 | |
| BOX 1 | |
| BOX 2 | |
| BOX 3 | |
| BOX 4 | |
| BOX 5 | |
| BOX 6 | |
| BOX 7 | |
| BOX 8 | |
| BOX 9 | |
| BOX 10 | |
| BOX 11 | |
| BOX 12 | |
| BOX 13 | |
| BOX 14 | |
| BOX 15 | |

# 16-Ending
# Goal Chart

| | | | |
|---|---|---|---|
| BOX 0 | | BOX 16 | |
| BOX 1 | | BOX 17 | |
| BOX 2 | | BOX 18 | |
| BOX 3 | | BOX 19 | |
| BOX 4 | | BOX 20 | |
| BOX 5 | | BOX 21 | |
| BOX 6 | | BOX 22 | |
| BOX 7 | | BOX 23 | |
| BOX 8 | | BOX 24 | |
| BOX 9 | | BOX 25 | |
| BOX 10 | | BOX 26 | |
| BOX 11 | | BOX 27 | |
| BOX 12 | | BOX 28 | |
| BOX 13 | | BOX 29 | |
| BOX 14 | | BOX 30 | |
| BOX 15 | | BOX 31 | |

You can download goal charts from my website or you can create your own.

Now get started and write! Goal charts are fun to fill in. So go ahead, write the next choice. And then the next. And when you are done, you will have completed a book!

## STICKING TO GOALS

When it comes to any project, there are a few good things to remember about sticking to goals.

### BREAK IT DOWN

When you break your big goal (writing an interactive adventure) down into smaller goals (writing a box), it makes anything seem possible. Walking up the stairs at your house takes a lot of energy. Walking up one step takes almost no energy. When you're trying to get motivated, walk up the staircase ONE STEP AT A TIME!

## CROSS IT OFF

Each time you cross one small step off your list, it gives you a sense of accomplishment, and it encourages you to do more. And when you cross one small step off your list, you can even say something silly like, "Look what I did!" (Yes, I really do this. It makes me feel amazing!)

## CELEBRATE

Celebrate every time you move closer to reaching your goal. The star stickers may feel silly, but they are a fun way to celebrate taking a step forward. Also, as you see them fill up, it will be really exciting! You can be like, "Look at all the words I have written! I am crushing this project!"

## THE TORTOISE WINS!

With goals, it's important to remember that you don't have to get it all done in one day! That's the whole point of setting up a schedule and tracking it. You have a plan. If you stick to your plan, you will reach the end. Think about the tortoise and the hare. The hare tries to finish the goal (winning the race) as fast as possible. And you know what? He gets distracted. He gets sidetracked. The tortoise takes his time and moves steadily ahead. And he gets there! He wins the race and reaches his goal. Sure, he might have small distractions here or there, but he keeps moving forward, one step at a time. And if you do this with your interactive adventure (or any goal you make), it will be awesome!

*Slow and steady wins the race!*

# SOME FINAL THOUGHTS AS YOU WRITE

There are a few things to keep in mind as you write your amazing interactive adventure.

## KEEP READERS GUESSING

When you're writing your story, there are a couple ways you can think about it. First, you may be writing a story about making the right choices in life, and only by making all the right choices (stay in school, don't be a bully, don't talk back to your parents, do your chores, eat your vegetables) will you reach the end successfully. It's great if you want to write a book where making the logical and correct choices will lead to a positive ending and making bad choices will lead to your reader's demise.

But . . .

You don't have to write your interactive adventure that way.

What I'm saying is that it's sometimes fun to keep your reader guessing.

- Go down the dark, scary, tunnel or stay out in the safe, bright sunlight? Maybe going down the dark, scary tunnel is the path to a positive ending and staying out in the bright sunlight makes it easier for a zombie to see you and eat your brain.
- Jump in the water filled with flesh-eating piranhas or try to paddle your sinking boat to the shore? Maybe if you try to paddle your boat to the shore, you get captured by pirates, but if you jump in the water with the flesh-eating piranhas, you are able to dive down deep enough, and you find an underwater grotto.

You see what I'm saying? There are so many options. So many possibilities. What the reader "thinks" will get them to safety does not have to lead to safety. Sometimes it's better if it doesn't.

So, what I'm trying to say is:

**IT'S FUN TO KEEP THE READER GUESSING!**

## DON'T RUSH THE PLANNING

When I'm working on a project around the house, like remodeling a bathroom or building a deck, the hardest parts of the project are planning and cleaning up. I'm always so excited to get started. I want to see results. And when I'm "done," I want to kick back with a nice glass of iced tea and relax and look at all I've accomplished.

The same is true with writing any book, but especially with writing an interactive adventure. I get a great idea for a story. I want to write it!

But . . .

I have to take my time and plan it out.

You know from reading this book (you did read the book, right?) that planning takes the most time when it comes to interactive adventures. But if you actually take the time to plan it all out, the writing becomes a piece of cake (virtual cake, of course). The best thing you can do is tell yourself that planning will take a while, but that all this effort you put in now will pay off later when writing is so easy. Be prepared for it. Then take your time and do it.

*Have yourself a slice of virtual cake.*

*Oh wait, the cake is a lie.*

*Not sure what that means? Search it up on the internet.*

## HAVE FUN!

Reading interactive adventures is fun. Writing them is really fun, too!

Writing *can* be fun, and an interactive adventure is a way to make writing really enjoyable for kids and adults of all ages. The writing is short. The focus is on adventure. There are steps you can follow to get from the start of your story to the end. There are so many possibilities when it comes to story ideas.

Don't get caught up in trying to make everything perfect. Instead, just enjoy the process. Use your creative mind to come up with an interactive adventure that is totally unique to you.

Then let someone else read it . . .

. . . again, and again . . . and again.

# ABOUT THE AUTHOR

P. J. (Tricia) Hoover wanted to be a Jedi, but when that didn't work out, she became an electrical engineer instead. After a fifteen year bout designing computer chips for a living, P. J. started creating worlds of her own. She's the award-winning author of *PROBLEM SOLVERS: 15 Innovative Women Engineers and Coders,* and *Tut: The Story of My Immortal Life,* featuring a fourteen-year-old King Tut who's stuck in middle school. Under the Connor Hoover pseudonym she is also the author of the popular *Pick Your Own Quest* series, which are *Choose Your Own Adventure* style interactive adventures perfect for everyone. When not working on her own writing, P. J. writes science curriculum articles and edits amazing manuscripts for other authors. P. J. loves spending time practicing kung fu, fixing things around the house, and solving Rubik's cubes. For more information about P. J. (Tricia) Hoover, please visit her website
www.pjhoover.com.

Made in the USA
Coppell, TX
10 April 2022

76326909R00070